The Won World of Inventions

Written by Joanna Brundle
Designed by Daniel Scase

©Published 2022.
BookLife Publishing Ltd.
King's Lynn, Norfolk PE30 4LS

ISBN 978-1-80155-156-4

All rights reserved. Printed in Poland.
A catalogue record for this book is available
from the British Library.

The Wonderful World of Inventions
Written by Joanna Brundle. Adapted by William Anthony
Designed by Daniel Scase

An Introduction to Accessible Readers...

Our 'really readable' Accessible Readers have been specifically created to support the reading development of young readers with learning differences, such as dyslexia.

Our aim is to share our love of books with children, providing the same learning and developmental opportunities to every child.

INCREASED FONT SIZE AND SPACING improves readability and ensures text feels much less crowded.

OFF-WHITE BACKGROUNDS ON MATTE PAPER improves text contrast and avoids dazzling readers.

SIMPLIFIED PAGE LAYOUT reduces distractions and aids concentration.

CAREFULLY CRAFTED along guidelines set out in the British Dyslexia Association's Dyslexia-Friendly Style Guide.

Additional images courtesy of Shutterstock.com. 4-5 – Fasttailwind, MillaF. 6-7 – www.vivoscuola.it, Commodore Grace M. Hopper. 8-9 – HodagMedia, ilmarinfoto. 10-11 – Feng Yu, HDesert. 12-13 – Glen Bowman, Tiger Images. 14-15 – metamorworks, drserg. 16-17 – gary718, Rico Shen. 18-19 – ifong, Daniel Brasil. 20-21 – Natali Zakharova, Acroterion. 22-23 – Radio-Electronics staff, Avery Slack, methodshop.com. 24-25 – Roger Uttin, Steve Mann. 26-27 – New Africa, Juan Ci. 28-29 – Pangog200, Riccardo Mayer. 30 - metamorworks.

Contents

Inventors and Inventions

Inventions are completely new things. The people who have the ideas and create these inventions are called inventors.

Some inventions make our lives easier. Others keep us safe or help us to keep in touch with one another.

Almost everything you see, from paper to computers, has been invented by someone who had a clever idea for how to make our lives easier or more fun. People have been inventing things for thousands of years.

Famous Inventors

Some inventors stand out from the rest because they invented so many things. Leonardo da Vinci invented lots of incredible machines. In 1495 it's thought that he may have built a type of robot knight!

Grace Hopper was an American mathematician and part of the US Navy. Hopper invented some clever technology that let computers understand instructions. This changed how computers worked forever. Hopper also helped make the first computer you could buy in shops.

Moving Around

Have you ever thought about what the first bicycle looked like?

At the end of the 1800s, inventor James Starley created a type of penny-farthing bicycle. Penny-farthings had large front wheels and small back wheels.

Some inventions have made cars safer.

Windscreen wipers were invented in 1903 by Mary Anderson. The idea came to her on a snowy car journey when her driver had to keep stopping to clear snow from the screen.

At Home

Have you ever tried to walk around your house in the dark? If so, you'll understand why the invention of the light bulb was so important!

In 1879, Thomas Edison perfected the light bulb. It was bright and lasted a long time.

In 1947, Valerie Hunter Gordon began making nappies that could be thrown away. She used cotton wool with a cover made from old parachutes. Her idea was developed in the 1950s and her nappies soon went on sale.

Chocolate

Did you know that chocolate was only a drink before it became a sweet snack?

In 1847, Joseph Fry mixed sugar with cocoa butter and cocoa powder and pressed the mixture into moulds to set. These became the first chocolate bars.

Did you know chocolate chip cookies were invented by accident?

In 1938, Ruth Wakefield ran out of cocoa powder while making chocolate cookies. Instead, she used broken chunks of chocolate. The chunks didn't melt and she had accidentally invented chocolate chip cookies!

The Internet

A group of computers all linked together is called a network. The internet is a giant network of computers that share information. It began in 1969 as a network of just four computers in the United States, called ARPANET.

Computer scientist Tim Berners-Lee realised that a worldwide network of computers would connect people around the world. He invented something to help computers share information. His invention became known as the World Wide Web.

Communicating

Before telephones and emails were invented, people had to write letters. Unlike today, the person receiving the letter had to pay. In 1837, Rowland Hill invented a sticky stamp that was paid for by the person sending the letter instead.

The first handheld mobile phone was invented by Martin Cooper. It was launched in 1984. Because it was so big and heavy, it soon became known as 'The Brick'.

Lucky Accidents

Corn flakes were invented when John and Will Kellogg accidentally left boiled wheat to go stale. Instead of wasting it, they passed it through machines called rollers, which made flakes. They then tried again with corn. Corn flakes became very popular.

George de Mestral invented Velcro after a lucky accident in 1955. The prickly heads of certain plants had got stuck on his trousers and in his dog's fur during a walk. After seeing this, he invented a hook fastener, which we now call Velcro.

An engineer named Percy Spencer was working on special machines in 1945, when he noticed that a peanut bar in his pocket had started to cook. He then tried the same thing with popcorn and an egg. They both exploded!

Spencer realised that the food had been quickly cooked from the inside by the microwaves from the special machines. He then designed the first working microwave oven. It was huge, weighing over 300 kilograms and standing 1.8 metres tall.

24
Radar
Range

Weird and Wacky

Some inventions are simply weird and wacky!

The Man from Mars Radio Hat was designed in 1949 by Victor Hoeflich. In the days before portable speakers, this hat let the person wearing it listen to music on the radio anywhere.

The Anti-theft Lunch Bag is a clear plastic bag printed with a picture of mould on it. It makes the sandwich inside look mouldy so that nobody will want to steal it!

The Sinclair C5 was like a car, but for just one person. It was a big failure because it didn't protect anyone from wind or rain. People also did not feel safe driving it.

Although it was a failure, the C5 made people begin to think about using electricity to power a car. Electric cars are much better for the planet than non-electric cars.

Young Inventors

Many inventions were created by young people.

Louis Braille was blind from a young age. This meant he could not see. When he was 15, he invented a way of reading and writing called braille.

Braille uses six bumps in different patterns. Each pattern means a different letter, number or symbol. A person can run their fingertips over the dotted patterns to read.

Many people around the world do not have clean water that is safe to drink.

Deepika Kurup was born in 1998. She invented a way to clean water with a material that uses sunlight to make water safer to drink.

Her invention doesn't cost too much money to use. This means it could bring clean drinking water to people all around the world. This means people are less likely to become ill because of drinking unsafe water.

Index:

The Wonderful World of Inventions: Quiz

1. What is an invention?

2. What did Louis Braille invent?

3. Which type of chocolate was invented first: the drink or the snack?

4. Can you use the contents page to find information about inventions that happened by accident?

5. Can you use the index to find a page in the book about food?

Helpful Hints for Reading at Home

This 'really readable' Accessible Reader has been carefully written and designed to help children with learning differences whether they are reading in the classroom or at home. However, there are some extra ways in which you can help your child at home.

- Try to provide a quiet space for your child to read, with as few distractions as possible.

- Try to allow your child as much time as they need to decode the letters and words on the page.

- Reading with a learning difference can be frustrating and difficult. Try to let your child take short, managed breaks between reading sessions if they begin to feel frustrated.

- Build your child's confidence with positive praise and encouragement throughout.

- Your child's teacher, as well as many charities, can provide you with lots of tips and techniques to help your child read at home.